Calling all amateur astronomers and star-gazers! You don't have to be an expert to check out the solar system. Through a small telescope, you can see the celestial bodies better than Galileo did with his instruments. In these circles, we see the Sun, Moon, and planets as they would appear through the eyepiece of a telescope at 100 power.

Sun

Moon

Mars

Jupiter

Mercury

Venus

Saturn

Uranus

Neptune

PLANETS

The Latest View of the Solar System

DAVID A. AGUILAR

NATIONAL
GEOGRAPHIC
WASHINGTON, D.C.

First Scholastic Edition
ISBN 978-1-4263-0898-7

**The Library of Congress
has cataloged the hard-
cover editons as follows:**

Aguilar, David A.
13 planets : the latest view
of the solar system / by
David A. Aguilar.
   p. cm.
 Includes bibliographical
references and index.
 ISBN 978-1-4263-0770-6
(hardcover : alk. paper) –
ISBN 978-1-4263-0771-3
(lib. bdg. : alk. paper)
 1. Solar system–Juvenile literature. 2. Planets–Juvenile
literature. I. Title. II. Title:
Thirteen planets.
QB501.3.A384 2011
523.2--dc22

2010032510

Illustration Credits
All artwork & photography
by David Aguilar unless other-
wise noted below:

Ju-Seok, Choi: 47 (top),
49 (top);
Stocktrek Images/ Corbis:
2 (background), 61;
NASA: 22 (all), 29 (all), 35 (all),
38 (all), 43 (bottom), 51 (earth);
Michael Hampshire/
NationalGeographicStock.com:
31 (top), 51 (top);
Michael Whelan/
NationalGeographicStock.com:
15 (top), 17 (top), 19 (top), 21
(top), 27 (top), 33 (top), 37
(top), 41 (top), 43 (top),
45 (top)

Printed in USA
11/WOR/1

CONTENTS

Foreword 9 The Latest View of the Solar System 10
How Our Solar System Formed 12
The Sun 15

1 MERCURY 17

2 VENUS 19

3 EARTH 21
Earth's Moon 22 *Meteorites* 24

4 MARS 27
Water on Mars 28

5 CERES / ASTEROID BELT 31

6 JUPITER 33
Jupiter's Moons 34

7 SATURN 37
Saturn's Moons 38

8 URANUS 41

9 NEPTUNE 43

10 PLUTO 45

11 HAUMEA / KUIPER BELT 47

12 MAKEMAKE 49

13 ERIS / DWARFS 51

Comets / Oort Cloud 52
The End of Our Solar System 54 Other Solar Systems 56

Glossary 58 *Planet Charts* 58 *The Solar System in a Grocery Bag* 59
Acknowledgments 60 *Further Exploration* 60 *Index* 60

FOREWORD

Once upon a time, long ago and far away, there were precisely seven planets: Moon, Mercury, Venus, Sun, Mars, Jupiter, and Saturn, all apparently revolving around a solidly fixed Earth. And then about five centuries ago came Nicholas Copernicus, who invented the solar system. He said the Sun was really in the middle surrounded by six planets: Mercury, Venus, Earth (with Moon), Mars, Jupiter, and Saturn. It was truly the Sun's system, with Earth now a spinning planet. It was all very simple and elegant.

Three centuries after Copernicus, things were no longer so simple. In 1781 another big planet, Uranus, was found, and then a lot of small ones were given names like Ceres, Astraea, Flora, Hygeia, and Kalliope. In 1846, still another big planet, Neptune, gained planetary status. By 1854 there were 41 planets, and astronomers cried "Enough!" So they all decided there were eight large planets, and the little guys weren't really planets but minor planets.

Today astronomers know that the solar system is much more complex and interesting than anyone dreamed of in the 1850s. There are more than 130 natural satellites, and more are being discovered. One, Saturn's Titan, is bigger than the planet Mercury. If Titan and our moon had independent orbits, they would qualify as planets. Astronomers now have orbits for nearly 500,000 minor planets, half of which have been assigned numbers, and about 15,000 of which have been given names. Almost all of them are irregularly-shaped rocks, but at least one, Ceres, is massive enough for its gravity to pull it into a sphere, so it is a dwarf planet.

And there are the comets, hoards of them in the deep freeze beyond Neptune. Occasionally some of these huge chunks of dirty ice get nudged into the inner parts of the solar system, where they thaw out and sprout long, beautiful tails. And a few of these ice balls are massive enough to pull themselves into spherical dwarf planets. Pluto is one of these, smaller than our moon. Makemake and Haumea are still smaller, while Eris is a little larger than Pluto. Three of these even have their own satellites. Undoubtedly more of these icy dwarf planets await discovery.

For now, there are eight classical planets and five dwarf planets, making thirteen!

DR. OWEN GINGERICH
Former Research Professor
of Astronomy,
Harvard and Astronomer
Emeritus, Smithsonian
Astronomical Observatory
August 2010

Our Sun is a medium-size light yellow star. Its gravity holds 13 planets plus countless asteroids and icy comets that circle around it. The planets are divided into three groups based on size, how tightly packed together they are (density), and what they are made of (composition). In orbits close to our Sun we find the small, dense, rocky worlds of Mercury, Venus, Earth, and Mars. They are called the terrestrial planets—the Latin word *terra* means "land." Past Mars

Ceres

Mars

Earth

Venus

Mercury

Jupiter

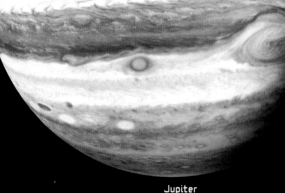

Sun

is the asteroid belt—an area filled with rocky leftovers from the time our solar system formed. Hiding out inside the asteroid belt is a new type of planet— a dwarf planet—named Ceres. Located beyond the asteroid belt are the gas giants—Jupiter, Saturn, Uranus, and Neptune. They are monster worlds made of frozen gases surrounded by rings and numerous moons. Beyond the gas giants is the Kuiper Belt—an area filled with comets and other objects. The Kuiper Belt also contains four other dwarf planets: Pluto, Haumea, Makemake, and Eris.

This artwork shows the relative sizes of the 13 planets but not the distances between them. Using the planet sizes shown here, the Sun would be about 40 inches (100 cm) in diameter and dwarf planet Eris would be some 7,750 yards (7,083 m) away. That's 580 large school buses lined up bumper to bumper or 77 football fields!

Saturn

Uranus

Neptune

Pluto

Haumea

Makemake

Eris

About five billion years ago, a huge star exploded into a supernova. This explosion sent shock waves rippling through space, creating a swirling cloud of gas and stardust. As the cloud spun faster and faster, it formed disks with glowing red bulges at their centers. One of those bulges began to slowly heat up and eventually became our Sun.

At the same time, not far from this bulge, bits of dust and rock containing carbon, silicon, and ice smashed together to form small objects called planetesimals. These soon merged into the terrestrial, or rocky, planets like Earth. Located close to the Sun, these worlds were rich in metals like the ones we use to build bridges and cars.

In the outer reaches of space, larger planets like Jupiter and Saturn collected ice, hydrogen, and methane gas to become gas giants. Beyond these frozen worlds, the dwarf planets formed out of ice and rock.

Wherever astronomers point their telescopes, they can see new solar systems forming. Some have thick dust rings shaped like doughnuts with baby planets hidden deep inside them. Other stars have thin dust rings with open spaces where new planets have already come together. Today, we have identified more than a thousand new planets circling distant stars, as well as 47 new solar systems around distant stars. The number of newly discovered planets will increase to the thousands in the next few years. Maybe one of these planets will resemble our own Earth.

Swirling
clouds of gas
and stardust

Dust disk
forming

Planetesimals
growing into
planets

Our solar
system today

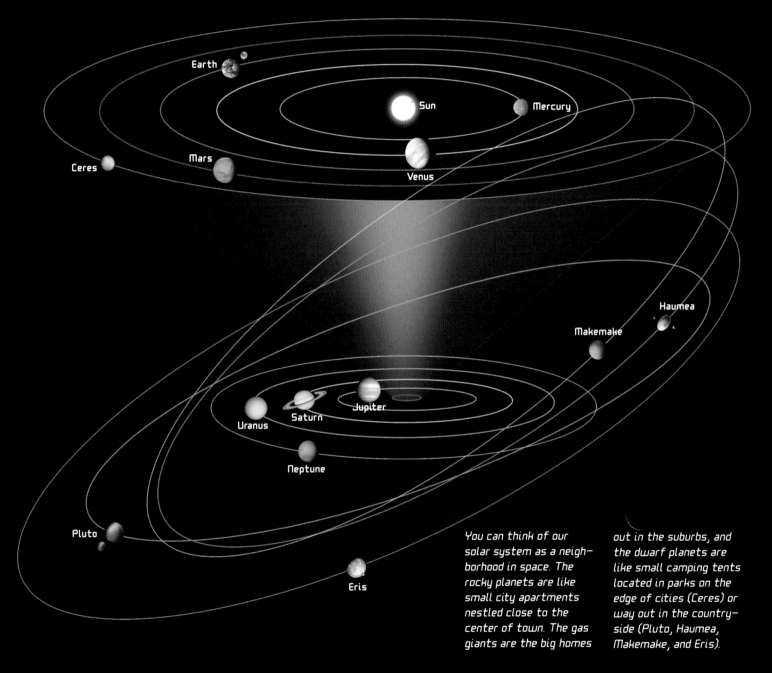

You can think of our
solar system as a neigh-
borhood in space. The
rocky planets are like
small city apartments
nestled close to the
center of town. The gas
giants are the big homes
out in the suburbs, and
the dwarf planets are
like small camping tents
located in parks on the
edge of cities (Ceres) or
way out in the country-
side (Pluto, Haumea,
Makemake, and Eris).

13

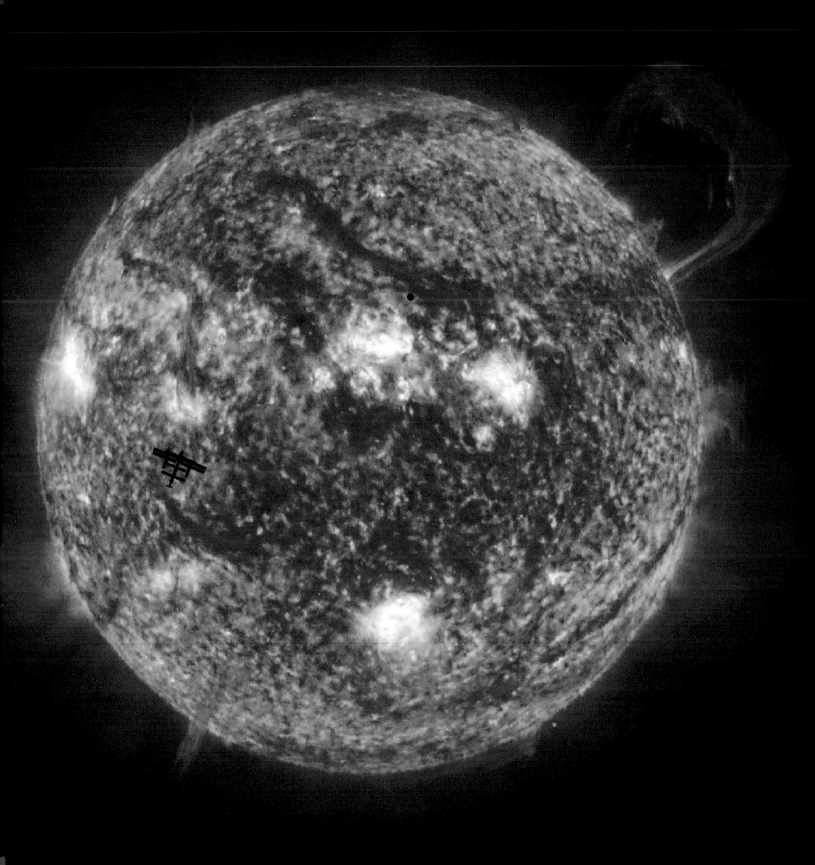

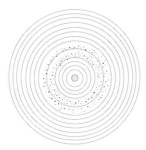

The Sun: Center of our solar system

Here's a trick question for your parents: What is the closest star to Earth? It's the Sun! With its tremendous gravity, this yellow star anchors the solar system together. It is also the energy source that makes life possible here on Earth. The surface of the Sun averages about 10,000°F (5500°C). It is a huge ball of burning gas comprised of 74 percent hydrogen, 25 percent helium (the same gas as in party balloons), and one percent heavy elements like iron and uranium that were created during violent explosions of ancient stars.

Our Sun is a third-generation star. All of the heavier elements that are found inside the Sun, in Earth, and even in our own bodies are part of two other stars that came and went ages ago. Isn't it amazing to know that everything in our solar system is made from recycled stardust?

Viewed through special solar filters, we witness two solar crossings: Mercury (upper black dot) and the International Space Station as they pass in front of this blinding ball of heat and light. Just one solar flare, like the one on the right, can unleash more energy than all the atomic bombs ever detonated.

In ancient Greece and Rome, the Sun was the mightiest of all the gods. The Greeks named him Apollo. Apollo was life-giver to Earth and patron god of musicians and poets. Sunday is named in honor of the Sun.

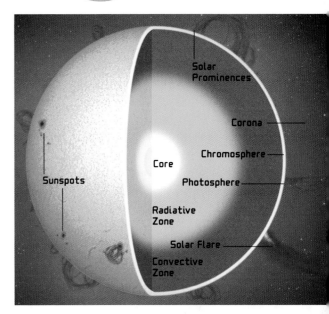

Solar Prominences

Corona

Chromosphere

Core

Photosphere

Sunspots

Radiative Zone

Solar Flare

Convective Zone

The bright surface of the Sun is called the photosphere, where sunspots, loops of gas called prominences, and explosive solar flares occur. The Sun's core is the nuclear furnace that sends heat out through the radiative zone, the convective zone, and the chromosphere until it reaches the surface. This process takes about one million years. Then, just nine minutes later, we feel the warmth here on Earth.

Mercury: First planet from the Sun

Mercury is a dead planet and the most heavily cratered object in our solar system. It is a world of black starry skies, gray craters, no moon, and not enough gravity to hold an atmosphere. Without an atmosphere, Mercury is a silent world without any sound. Big cracks on the surface indicate this planet is still shrinking as its hot iron core grows cold. Mercury races around the Sun in 88 Earth days but spins so slowly on its axis that it takes 176 Earth days from sunrise to sunset. On this planet, a year is shorter than a day! The daytime side exposed to the Sun for six months sizzles with a temperature of 800°F (427°C). This is hot enough to melt lead or set your house on fire. On the night side, frozen temperatures drop to a chilling -300°F (-183°C) making Mercury one of the hottest and coldest places in our solar system at the same time.

Like our Moon, Mercury is pitted and scarred by craters, sharp cliffs, and ancient lava flows. Most sky observers never see Mercury because it orbits so close to the Sun that it's lost in the glare of our star.

With wings on his helmet and heels, Mercury was the speedy messenger of the Roman gods. In the languages that come from Latin (including French, Italian, and Spanish), Wednesday is named after him (mer-credi, mercoledì, and miércoles, respectively).

Almost 900 miles (1,450 km) in diameter, the yellow-colored Caloris Basin formed four billion years ago when an asteroid 60 miles (97 km) in diameter smashed into Mercury at ten times the speed of a bullet. Shock waves pushed up jumbled mountains about a mile and a half (2.4 km) high on the opposite side of the planet.

17

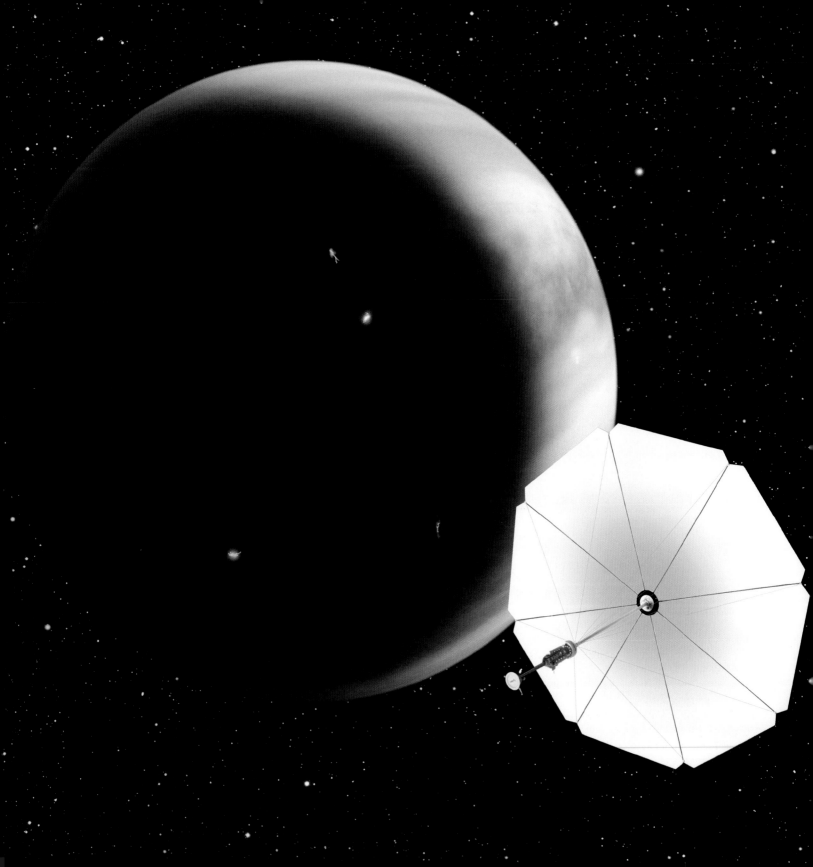

Venus: Second planet from the Sun

Bright enough to cast shadows on Earth at night, Venus has long been considered Earth's "twin." Both planets are about the same size and are made out of the same materials. However, surrounded by clouds of deadly sulfuric acid 40 miles (65 km) thick, lit by 100–million–volt lightning bolts, and covered by thousands of volcanoes, Venus might be considered Earth's evil twin. Trapping incoming sunlight with a runaway greenhouse effect, these clouds create surface temperatures of 870°F (465°C) that would melt lead. These blistering temperatures make Venus the hottest planet in the solar system. With the densest atmosphere of any planet, the weight pushing down on the surface could crush a submarine, and a slight breeze on the surface could roll an astronaut over like a powerful ocean wave. Venus may be almost the same size as Earth, but nothing else about it resembles our beautiful blue planet.

Powered by the steady solar winds, a majestic solar sail passes by Venus. On the nighttime side of this forbidding planet, the flashes of lightning light up the dark clouds. These bolts never reach the surface below.

Venus was the Roman goddess of love, beauty, and springtime. The symbol for her bright shining planet is the hand mirror. Friday is her day of the week. The word for Friday in many languages means "Venus's day."

As a future space probe hovers over Venus's dimly lit surface, the planet's barren volcanic landscape glows an eerie red. Higher than Mount Everest, the distant volcano Maxwell Montes rises almost 7 miles (11 km) above this deadly alien landscape.

EARTH

Earth: Third planet from the Sun

Between Venus and Mars, a special planet formed that would eventually have oceans, land, and life. This third planet from the Sun shines like a blue gem in space with an oxygen-rich atmosphere created by microscopic plants. Spinning on its axis at 1,000 miles an hour (1,600 kph), it takes 365 days to make one complete trip around the Sun. Located at just the right distance from our star, it is the only planet where water exists as a liquid, as a solid (ice), and as a vapor (in clouds). With the most diverse terrain of any planet, the hard outer crust is just a thin layer covering a molten interior. In fact, if we could shrink Earth down to the size of an apple, the ground we walk on would be as thin as an apple peel. Yet, on this beautiful world, life thrives everywhere—under the seas, inside rocks, on mountains, in deserts, and even high up in the atmosphere.

No other planet resembles Earth. Blue and white from its oceans and clouds, our planet is teeming with life. In this artwork you can see both Earth and its companion Moon with the shadowed lines that divide night from day.

Gaea, the Earth goddess of the ancient Greeks, was known as the mother of Earth. Born out of chaos, she in turn gave birth to the sky, the seas, and the land. The Romans called her Terra.

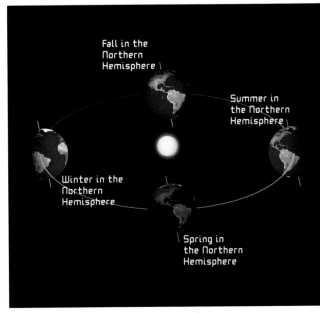

Fall in the Northern Hemisphere

Summer in the Northern Hemisphere

Winter in the Northern Hemisphere

Spring in the Northern Hemisphere

Seasonal changes are caused by the 23.5-degree tilt of Earth on its axis, not by how close it is to the Sun. When the Northern Hemisphere is tipped toward the Sun, it is summertime there and winter in the Southern Hemisphere. Six months later, when the Southern Hemisphere is tipped toward the Sun, it is summertime there and winter in the Northern Hemisphere.

The closest celestial neighbor to Earth is covered with huge craters, rugged mountains, and flat, dark gray plains formed from lava that once flowed across its surface billions of years ago. Formed from chunks of Earth that blasted into space when an object the size of Mars hit it, the Moon was too small to have the gravity necessary to hold on to an atmosphere—life never got started. But recently astronomers made a major discovery that will make future astronauts happy: Water was found on the polar regions of the Moon. Someday, astronauts will be able to collect this water, and using electricity, break it down into oxygen to breathe and hydrogen to make fuel for more exploration.

The gravity between Earth and the Moon have slowed the rotation of the Moon so that one side always faces Earth. The side of the Moon that faces us (the near side) is quite different from the side that faces away (the far side). The dark, flat plains we call Mare occur almost entirely on the near side. The Mare were caused by lava flowing out of ancient volcanoes and cooling. Scientists think the near side of the Moon had more volcanoes than the far side.

Near side with Mare

Far side with almost no Mare

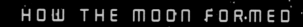

HOW THE MOON FORMED

1 During the early formation of our solar system, Earth collided with an object the size of Mars.

2 The debris that blasted into space formed a ring around Earth.

3 Quickly, the ring joined together and formed into our Moon. Thus, the Moon you see tonight is actually a part of our own planet Earth.

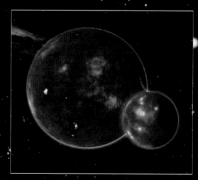

METEORITES

We see them streak across the sky at night. We may look up and say "Oh! A shooting star!" But what we see isn't really a star at all—it's a piece of rock or metal burning up in our atmosphere. Drifting through space, these objects are called meteoroids. When they enter a planet's atmosphere, they are superheated so much that they glow and are called meteors. When meteors hit the ground, they are called meteorites. Did you know the Earth gains almost a ton of weight every day from meteor dust drifting down from outer space? Most meteoroids are made of rock, but nearly 10 percent are made of nickel and iron. Occasionally a colossal meteorite strikes the Earth and leaves behind a gigantic crater.

Meteoroids need to start out at least the size of a golf ball to make it to the ground. If smaller, they vaporize and sprinkle down from the sky as dust. In fact, there might be meteorite dust on top of your dresser right now!

Periodic meteor showers, ones that occur the same time every year, can be spectacular. They're the remains of comets that have passed by Earth, leaving small pieces behind..

MARS

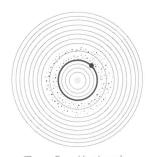

Mars: Fourth planet from the Sun

Fifty million miles farther out into space, we find Mars—the last terrestrial planet. Like a piece of iron left out in the rain, Martian soil has rusted red. That's why Mars is called the red planet. Half the diameter of Earth, Mars is a spectacular world. The canyon Valles Marinaris dwarfs anything found on Earth. Seen in the artwork at left, this canyon would stretch from New York to San Francisco. Mars has a volcano that stands 17 miles (27 km) high, large polar ice caps, and dust storms that can blanket the planet for months. Someday humans may live on Mars, but it won't be easy. The carbon dioxide atmosphere is so poisonous and cold that thin liquid water cannot exist on the surface. But if you like pink daytime skies, orange Martian sunsets, and vast desert scenery, Mars might be the perfect getaway for you!

Future explorers have fun on the Martian moon Phobos while a large dust storm breaks out on the southern Martian surface. At the ten o'clock position, we see the smaller and more distant companion moon, Deimos.

When Mars draws close to Earth, it appears blood red in color. This is why the Romans called Mars the god of war. His symbol is formed from a spear and shield. Tuesday is his day.

In the future, astronauts exploring Mars may release large floating platforms to map and explore the surface of the red planet. Looking down from above, the vast landscape passing underneath would be magnificent!

This is not the Mars we usually see in pictures today. When it first formed, it was covered with shallow lakes, flowing rivers, and vast oceans, making it a blue planet like Earth.

Mars is a world of deserts, craters, sand dunes, ancient riverbeds, rows of ancient volcanoes, and polar ice caps that shrink and grow as the seasons change. Although Mars is quite different from Earth, it remains one of the best places to look for extraterrestrial life in our solar system. Vast oceans may have once covered most of Mars. Four billion years ago, erupting volcanoes spewing sulfur gas into the atmosphere caused the oceans, lakes, and rivers to dry up. Today, Mars is one large, cold desert. However, new research indicates there may still be hidden pockets of water buried underground. Recently, primitive microbes taken from an Antarctic lake survived in laboratory experiments simulating conditions on Mars today. Who knows—life on Mars may still exist under the sands of the mysterious red planet.

1. Here we see layered ice deposits exposed in a cliff in the north polar region of Mars. These exposed layers help scientists study the history of the planet, and they reveal any recent climate changes that have occurred.

2. Looking straight down on Olympus Mons, we see the tallest and largest volcano in the solar system. Higher than three Mount Everests, it spans a larger area than all the Hawaiian Islands combined.

3. These dark trails are the paths of dust devils swirling across a sandy desert, exposing the darker basalt rock underneath. These dust devils can be 50 times larger than tornadoes on Earth. However, because the atmosphere on Mars is so thin, the dust devils are as weak as an afternoon breeze blowing through your window.

4. In this half-mile-wide (1 km) crater, we see sand dunes 200 feet (61 m) high crisscrossing the crater floor and trails of boulders the size of cars.

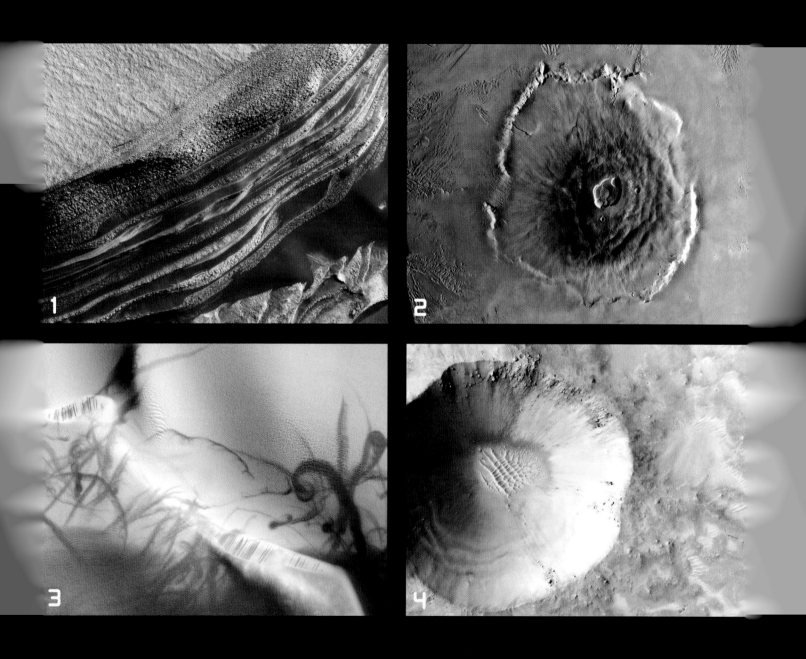

Ceres: Fifth planet
from the Sun

Astronomers were surprised when Ceres was discovered by accident in 1801. They immediately classified it as the fifth planet from the Sun, bumping Jupiter to sixth. In 1850 they changed their minds and reclassified it as an asteroid. In 2006 they decided it belonged in a new group of planets called dwarf planets. Hidden deep inside the asteroid belt, Ceres takes 4.6 Earth years to make one orbit around the Sun. About a quarter the diameter of our Moon, it is the largest object in the asteroid belt. Asteroids are really pieces of unfinished worlds leftover from the early solar system. Collisions frequently occur between these rocky leftovers. Occasionally, Jupiter's gravity nudges an asteroid out of its orbit and sends it toward the Sun. Very rarely, a big one hits Earth, which can be disastrous. Just ask the unlucky dinosaurs!

Dwarf planet Ceres (top right in the artwork) is part of the asteroid belt between Mars and Jupiter. It is the biggest of thousands of objects left in this area from the formation of the solar system.

Ceres was the Roman goddess of fruit, vegetables, and agriculture. Her symbol is the curved scythe—the tool used to cut grains for the harvest.

The asteroids are rich in metals. Someday, space miners may dock with an asteroid like Eros (shown in this artwork) to harvest these pure metals and send them back to Earth. What might an asteroid be worth? A solid nickel-iron asteroid one mile (1.6 km) in diameter is worth an estimated 12 trillion dollars!

JUPITER

Jupiter: Sixth planet from the Sun

Jupiter is the largest planet in our solar system. All the other planets could easily fit inside it. With at least 63 moons, Jupiter is almost a miniature solar system itself. This planet is made of hydrogen and helium gas with methane mixed in, so there is no solid surface to walk on. Jupiter's skies are blanketed by slushy frozen clouds filled with brilliant flashes of lightning and a giant Earth-size hurricane called the Great Red Spot. Radiating more than twice the amount of heat it collects from the Sun and spinning around once every ten hours, Jupiter bulges in the middle and smells terrible. The colorful brownish red stripes are made of ammonia hydrosulfide, which smells like rotten eggs. The white clouds are made of ammonia, so they smell like strong window cleaner. Jupiter also has rings circling it, but they are too thin to be seen from Earth.

The frozen surface of Jupiter's moon, Europa, is a perfect place to view the Great Red Spot—a hurricane that has raged for hundreds of years. Fed by smaller storms, this spinning hurricane never seems to stop.

Jupiter generates one of the strongest magnetic fields in the solar system. This magnetic field bends energy particles from the Sun, resulting in a beautiful green aurora that dances over Jupiter's north pole.

When Galileo first looked at Jupiter with his telescope, he couldn't believe his eyes. Four bright star-like objects formed a perfect line with the planet. Over the next few nights, these pinpoints of light changed their positions along this straight line. Galileo realized at once—Jupiter had moons! This discovery helped convince Galileo that people of his time were wrong to believe everything in the universe circled around Earth.

Did you know that four of Jupiter's largest moons can be seen with a pair of binoculars? Discovered by Galileo in 1610, they're called the Galilean moons. Io is the closest to Jupiter. Though only the size of our own Moon, Io is home to more than 150 volcanoes, which makes it the most geologically active object in our solar system. Europa is the second closest Galilean moon to Jupiter. Slightly smaller than Io, it has an icy surface that may cover a saltwater ocean. The third moon out from Jupiter is Ganymede—the largest moon in our solar system. The dark regions are old ice covered by dust. The white spots are places where meteorite impacts have exposed newer ice. The fourth Galilean moon is battered and bruised Callisto. Scientists are not sure if a liquid ocean lies under the ice or if this moon is just frozen solid.

1. The surface of Io looks more like a pizza than a moon. The red, orange, and yellow colors are layers of sulfur and lava from active volcanoes. Because Io is located so close to Jupiter, it has no ice or water.

2. Underneath Europa's icy surface may be a warm saltwater ocean up to 60 miles (100 km) deep. Someday, underwater hydrobots may explore this ocean looking for signs of life.

3. Ganymede is larger than the planets Mercury, Ceres, Pluto, and Eris combined. Its icy surface is covered with meteorite craters and dust, but underneath the surface may be a liquid ocean like Europa's.

4. Callisto is the most heavily cratered object in the solar system. Its surface was formed some four billion years ago. Unlike the other three Galilean moons, it doesn't have a molten core.

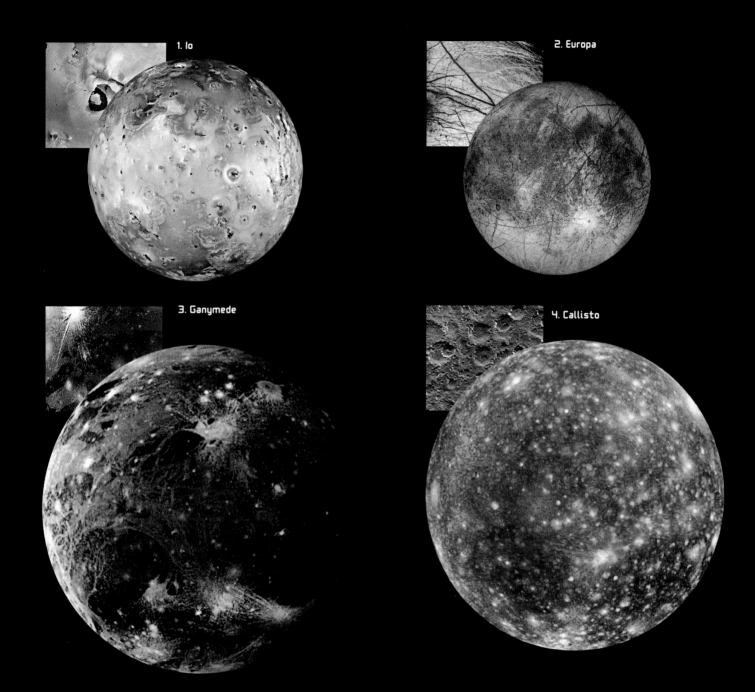

1. Io

2. Europa

3. Ganymede

4. Callisto

SATURN

Saturn: Seventh planet from the Sun

Saturn is the most distant planet visible to the naked eye. Like Jupiter, it has no surface to walk on. Its frozen slushy atmosphere, made mostly of hydrogen and helium gas, forms faint bands across its surface. Saturn's density is so low that if you dropped the planet into water, it would float like a cork. Consisting of thousands of individual little bands called ringlets, the most dazzling set of rings surrounds Saturn like a crown. Composed of particles ranging from dust grains to giant boulders, they are the remains of a small moon or asteroid that was torn apart hundreds of millions of years ago. The rings are brighter than Saturn itself. Astronomers divide them into seven different bands labeled A to G. If you ever have the chance to look at Saturn through a telescope, do it! No other planet in our solar system is quite as regal.

Looking over the giant crater Herschel on Saturn's moon Mimas, we can see just how thin the planet's rings are. If their diameter were reduced to the size of a football field, they would appear as thin as a piece of paper.

Because Saturn moves so slowly across the sky at night, the Romans associated it with the grandfather of the gods, Jupiter's father. The symbol for Saturn is the sickle—a tool used for cutting grain. Saturday is named for this planet.

This newly discovered, dark ring around Saturn is the largest known planetary ring in the solar system. If you could see it from Earth, Saturn would be a bright dot and the ring would be twice the diameter of the full moon.

Saturn has 62 confirmed moons in all sizes, shapes, and colors. The largest and most mysterious is Titan. Behind thick, rusty clouds, Titan may hold the key to the origin of life on Earth. Larger than the planet Mercury or any of the dwarf planets, Titan has a thick atmosphere, drizzling rain, seasonal changes, and lakes of crude oil that may amount to more than all the crude oil found on Earth. The dense atmosphere is mostly nitrogen with orange-red ethane and methane clouds. This atmosphere closely matches the atmosphere on Earth four billion years ago when primitive life first started. Could there be extraterrestrial life on this distant cold moon where temperatures reach a "balmy" -290°F (-179°C)? Within your lifetime we may find the answer.

Smothered by layers of red and orange clouds, the landscape of Titan includes hydrocarbon lakes and rivers. It rains day in and day out on Titan, but instead of water, liquid methane drizzles down onto the surface, keeping it wet and slushy.

Titan

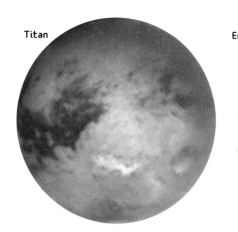

Titan is the only moon in the solar system with a thick, hazy atmosphere. Its frozen surface is spotted with dark lakes of liquid methane.

Enceladus

Coated with fine crystals of ice from erupting water volcanoes, Enceladus reflects almost 100 percent of the sunlight reaching it back into space.

Iapetus

With one hemisphere colored black and the other colored white, Iapetus is the only two-toned moon in the solar system.

Mimas

Rocked by a collision that almost destroyed it, Mimas's most distinctive feature is the impact crater Herschel, which is almost 80 miles (130 km) across.

URANUS

Uranus: Eighth planet from the Sun

Uranus glows like an aquamarine gem because of the methane gas in its atmosphere. Resembling a tiny green pea when viewed in an amateur telescope, this icy giant is about eight times the size of Earth. Unlike any other planet in our solar system, Uranus has a 98-degree tilt to its axis. Scientists think that early in its history the planet was hit by something really big that knocked it completely over on its side. Uranus's rings turned sideways, too. Viewed straight on, it looks like a bull's-eye in space. Right now, Uranus's north pole faces the Sun while its south pole faces away into space. This means the north pole is experiencing 42 years of sunlight, which will be followed by 42 years of darkness. There is no solid surface on Uranus. It is made mostly of hydrogen and helium gas like our Sun. Uranus has 27 moons, the third highest number of moons behind Jupiter and Saturn.

Some scientists believe the grooves on Uranus's moon Miranda (foreground) were caused by meteorite strikes that liquefied the subsurface ice, which then rose to the surface and refroze in a wavy pattern.

Uranus was named for the Greek god who was the father of Saturn and the grandfather of Jupiter. The symbol is the sign for the metal platinum. Uranus was discovered in 1781. Until then, people knew about only six planets.

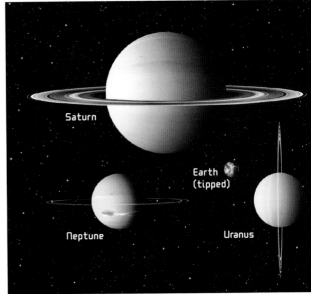

Saturn

Earth (tipped)

Neptune

Uranus

If Earth tipped on its side like Uranus, sunlight hitting the north pole would cause violent weather while the south pole would experience frigid darkness. Most life would be concentrated in a belt stretching around the Equator.

NEPTUNE

Neptune: Ninth planet from the Sun

Neptune is the smallest gas giant and the farthest from the Sun. It also has the wildest weather of any planet in the solar system, with winds that blow at speeds more than 1,200 miles an hour (2,000 kph). Like the rest of the gas giants, Neptune has no solid surface to walk on. The temperature at the top of the cloud layer is a chilling -350°F (-214°C). However, Neptune's core remains hotter than the Sun's surface. Internal heat bubbling up causes violent winds and hurricanes. Neptune was discovered using mathematical calculations. When astronomers realized something big was affecting the orbit of Uranus, they calculated where that object might be in space. When they searched, they found Neptune. Since its discovery more than 160 years ago, Neptune has yet to complete one full orbit around the Sun.

The blue methane clouds of Neptune reflect dim sunlight onto the frozen surface of its large moon Triton. Colder than Pluto, Triton's ice volcanoes spew frozen methane flakes across the moon's surface.

Neptune is the Roman god of the sea. This is fitting for a planet colored like the oceans. His symbol is the trident—an ancient fishing spear.

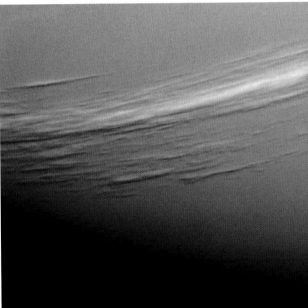

In its closest approach to Neptune, the Voyager 2 spacecraft snapped this picture of the tops of the clouds floating high in Neptune's atmosphere.

Scientists think diamonds may be created in the dense hot conditions that exist under the cloud tops of both Uranus and Neptune.

PLUTO

Pluto: Tenth planet from the Sun

For the last ten years of his life, Percival Lowell, the astronomer famous for believing he had discovered canals on Mars, searched for a "Planet X" beyond the orbit of Neptune. As hard as he tried, he never found it. In 1930, 14 years after Lowell's death, Clyde Tombaugh—a 22-year-old night assistant at the observatory named after Lowell—discovered Pluto. For 76 years Pluto was the ninth planet from the Sun. Then, in 2006 it was demoted to a dwarf planet and, with the addition of Ceres, became the tenth planet from the Sun. Because Pluto's moon Charon is so large, some astronomers consider Pluto and Charon a double-planet system. Located at the fringes of the Kuiper Belt, Pluto travels in an egg-shaped orbit around the Sun, sometimes crossing inside the orbit of Neptune to temporarily become the ninth planet from the Sun again.

Stars in the Milky Way help illuminate Pluto, its two smaller moons Nix and Hydra, and erupting ice volcanoes on its large moon Charon. In the distance, dust from the asteroid belt creates a fuzzy glow around the Sun.

Pluto was the Roman god of wealth and the underworld. The planet's symbol is a combination of the letters P and L. They stand for astronomer Percival Lowell, who searched for Pluto.

Pluto is one of the coldest objects in the solar system. When it reaches its farthest distance from the Sun, its atmosphere freezes and falls to the ground, where it looks like a thin coating of sugar frosting.

Haumea: Eleventh planet from the Sun

Located in the Kuiper (rhymes with "wiper") Belt, Haumea (Hah-oo-MAY-ah) is one of the most unusual objects in the solar system. It is as big across as Pluto but shaped more like a chicken egg. Some scientists have called the planet a "cosmic football" because it tumbles end over end like a football kicked for a field goal. Spinning once every four hours, Haumea is probably the result of an earlier collision that left this oblong shape behind and started its unusually rapid rotation. All the information we can gather tells us it is a solid rock with a glaze of shiny ice covering it. If you could cut it in half, it would remind you of an M&M. The outside candy coating is the ice and the chocolate found inside is the rock.

Haumea is the strangest shaped dwarf planet discovered so far. Shown here with its two small gray moons, Hi'iaka, at upper left and Namaka on the lower right, a strange splash of red color marks a part of its surface.

Haumea was named for a powerful Hawaiian sorceress who gave birth to many creatures on Earth. The planet's two moons were named after her daughters Hi'iaka and Namaka.

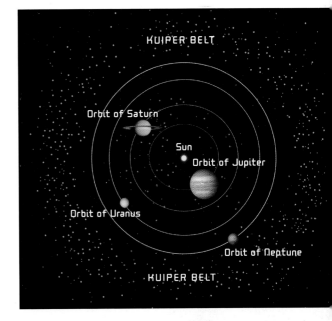

Past Neptune, we now enter the Kuiper Belt. Think of it as a larger version of the asteroid belt between Mars and Jupiter. This is where we find all the dwarf planets except Ceres. In this diagram, main Kuiper Belt objects are colored green. Scattered objects are colored orange.

47

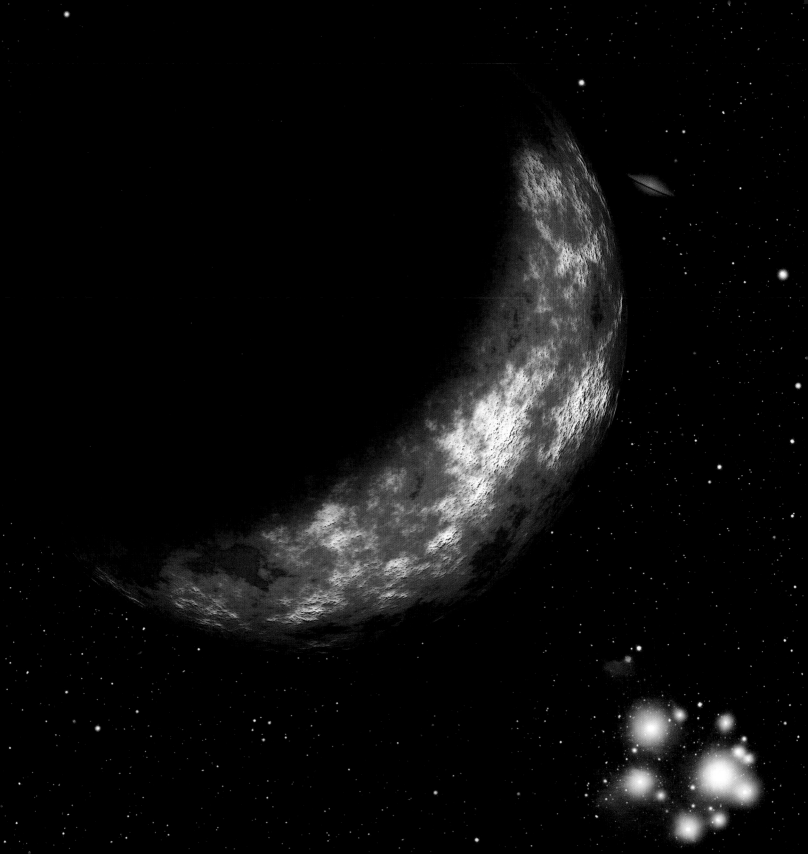

Makemake: Twelfth planet from the Sun

Makemake (MAH-keh MAH-keh) and Ceres are the only dwarf planets without moons. Discovered right around Easter in 2005, it was originally called "Easterbunny." It is the third largest dwarf planet found thus far, smaller than both Eris and Pluto. Methane and nitrogen gas have been detected in its atmosphere, leading scientists to believe the atmosphere might freeze and fall to the ground in wintertime, just like Pluto's atmosphere. That may be the reason it appears so bright in the sky. The Earth takes 365 days to orbit the Sun. Makemake's orbital period is 310 Earth years. We can't imagine how cold it is on the 12th planet because we don't have any comparable temperatures on Earth. On a "warm" day on Makemake, don't bother with summer clothes. Temperatures are -406°F (-240°C).

The oddly red-colored dwarf planet Makemake reflects just enough dim sunlight to be seen in large telescopes back on Earth. Off in the distance, the stunning open star cluster, the Pleiades, shines like sapphire jewels.

Makemake is named for the Easter Island God of fertility, creator of humans, and chief God of the bird-man cult. His image is carved on many of the rocks on the island.

Easter Island is a Polynesian island located far off the coast of Chile. Unlike all the classical planets that were named after Greek gods, Makemake is named in honor of the gods of the South Pacific Islands.

Eris: Thirteenth planet from the Sun

Eris is the coldest and most distant dwarf planet in our solar system with an orbit that is more oval than round. Larger than Pluto, it is made of one-third rock and two-thirds ice. With its moon Dysnomia, Eris passes through the Kuiper Belt and continues traveling ten billion miles (16 billion km) beyond it. Because it is larger than Pluto, its discoverers originally named it the solar system's tenth major planet. Today it is classified as a dwarf planet. Unlike reddish-colored Pluto and Makemake, Eris appears gray.

In the future, more dwarf planets will be added to our solar system list. In our universe, dwarf stars are the most common type of stars and dwarf galaxies are the most common type of galaxies. It makes sense that dwarf planets may be the most common type of planets out there, too.

The dwarf planet Eris and its moon, Dysnomia, orbit the farthest regions of our solar system. The discovery of Eris in 2005 started the debate that ultimately resulted in Pluto's reclassification as a dwarf planet.

Eris was the Roman goddess of discord or fighting. She was always causing trouble. Her symbol is the apple. Legend says when she threw a golden apple into a room, the resulting arguments caused the Trojan Wars.

Sedna

Orcus

Vanth

2007OR10

Weywot

Quaoar

Here are four Kuiper Belt objects that have been identified as future dwarf planet candidates. One does not have an official name yet. What would you name it?

Comets have been called the "dirty snowballs" of the solar system. The word "comet" comes from the Greek word *kometes*, which means "hairy star." Made of sand, water, ice, and carbon dioxide, comets can suddenly appear in our sky displaying long ghost-like tails. Halley's Comet, which returns in its travels around the Sun in less than 200 years, comes from the Kuiper Belt. However, comets like Hale-Bopp that take millions of years to complete one trip around the Sun, come from the Oort (rhymes with "port") Cloud. As comets draw nearer to the Sun, they begin to defrost. Solar energy vaporizes their ices, forming a glowing halo, or coma. Soon a long, spectacular tail blown by the solar winds may emerge, stretching for millions of miles across space. Some 800 comets have visited our skies in recorded history. There may be trillions more out in the Oort Cloud.

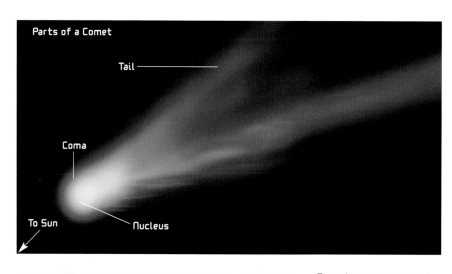

Parts of a Comet

Tail

Coma

Nucleus

To Sun

Astronomers believe the Oort Cloud is the remains of the solar nebula that collapsed to form our solar system. This cloud may extend halfway to the Sun's nearest star neighbor,

Proxima Centauri, which is shown on the lower right with an Oort cloud of its own. It would take 100,000 years for a space shuttle to fly from the Sun to Proxima Centauri.

Comets are composed of a tiny nucleus of rock and ice that becomes surrounded by a gaseous coma as it heats up. As a comet draws closer to our Sun, long separate tails of gas and dust can form—always pointing away from the Sun. Comets may be much more important than just a spectacular sight. An early bombardment of comets may have seeded a young Earth with water that fills our oceans and supplied the molecular building blocks that started life on our planet around 4 billion years ago.

There is an old saying: All good things must come to an end. That's fine for some things, but what if it's the end of Earth? That's a very different situation to think about! The key to all this is our Sun. When it formed around 4.6 billion years ago, it gathered enough hydrogen and helium gas to keep burning for about 12 billion years. Over time, the Sun has used part of that fuel to heat our planet and provide the energy for plants and animals to survive. In another billion years, our Sun will start to run short of hydrogen, resulting in an increase in brightness. This will heat up Earth like Venus. In time, all our oceans will boil away, the mountains will melt, and the Earth will look like a bowling ball. Five billion years later, the Sun will expand into a red giant, consuming Mercury, Venus, and maybe Earth. At 12 billion years of age, it will puff out a beautiful planetary nebula into space and then shrink back down, becoming a tiny white dwarf and eventually fading away.

Life will have disappeared from Earth when our Sun swells up into a red giant. If we can master space travel before this happens, it may present an opportunity for cosmic travelers from Earth to relocate to other Earth-like planets out among the stars.

Seven billion years into the future, this may be all that is left of our Earth and Moon as our Sun puffs out a beautiful red planetary nebula. This bubble of gas will remain visible for a time, leaving behind a white dwarf star.

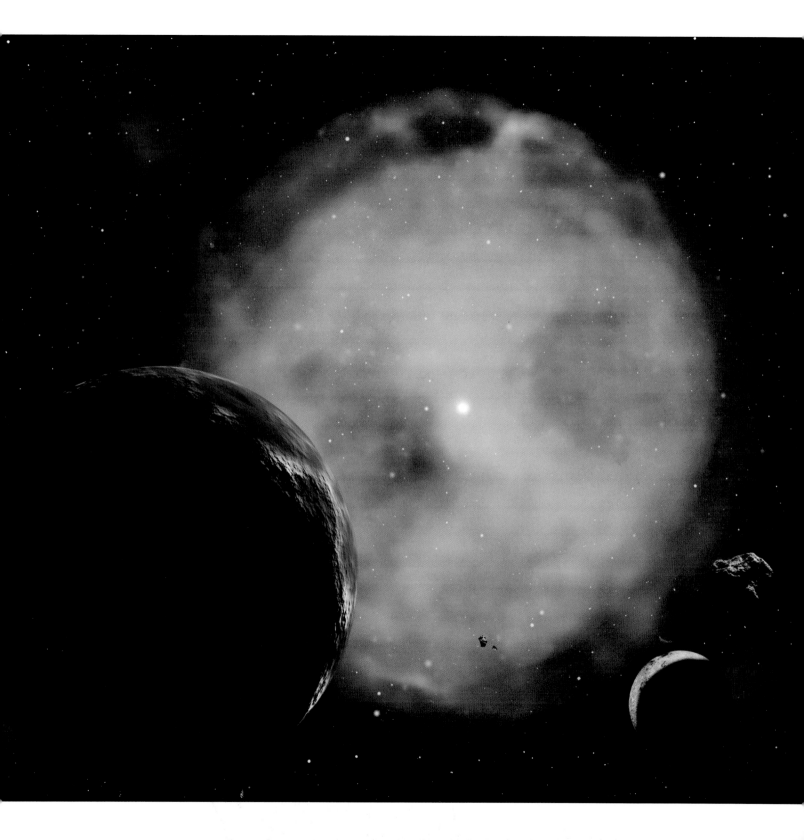

Beyond our solar system, astronomers have discovered more than a thousand new extrasolar planets orbiting nearby stars. Some are called "hot Jupiters" because they are gas giants orbiting closer to their stars than Mercury. We also have identified planets the size of Uranus and Neptune because they are big and easy to find. Soon, however, we will unveil the first Earthlike worlds in orbits around their stars that will permit liquid water to exist on their surfaces. Many of these worlds made of rock and ice will be a bit larger than our own planet. They will be called "super-Earths." In fact, we have found some already! The next challenge will be to determine if there is life there. Within the next twenty years, we may know this answer, too.

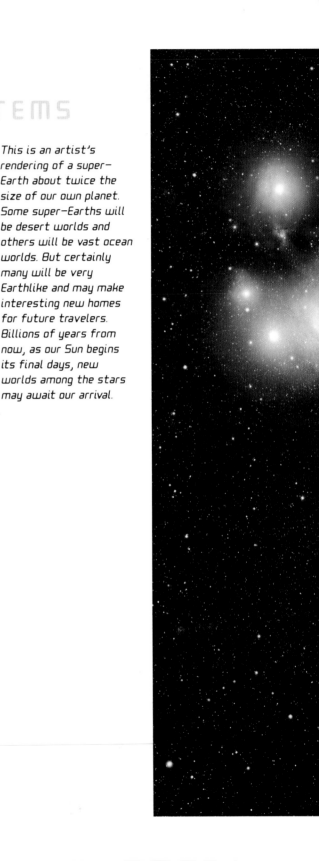

This is an artist's rendering of a super-Earth about twice the size of our own planet. Some super-Earths will be desert worlds and others will be vast ocean worlds. But certainly many will be very Earthlike and may make interesting new homes for future travelers. Billions of years from now, as our Sun begins its final days, new worlds among the stars may await our arrival.

Hot Jupiters are also called "roaster planets" because they orbit so close to their stars. In this artist's view, a hot Jupiter with an orbit of less than one Earth day leaves behind a comet-like tail as it zooms around its star.

Dwarf planet
One of a new class of small planets that includes Ceres, Pluto, Haumea, Makemake, and Eris.

Extrasolar planet
A planet that orbits a star other than our Sun.

Extraterrestrial life
Life originating outside Earth. Most scientists believe it exists, but none has yet been found.

Gas giant planet
One of a class of large planets composed mostly of frozen hydrogen, helium, and ices. The gas giant planets in our solar system are Jupiter, Saturn, Uranus, and Neptune. There is no surface or ground on a gas giant, so they would be impossible to walk on.

Greenhouse effect
The effect that occurs when gases in the atmosphere of a planet trap incoming heat from their sun and do not let it escape back into space. This causes the surface of the planet to heat up just like a green-house where tropical flowers are grown.

Hot Jupiter
A Jupiter-size extrasolar planet that orbits very close to its star, which makes it very hot. Hot Jupiters are the easiest extrasolar planets to detect from Earth.

Light-year
The distance light travels in a vacuum in one year. It equals 5,878,625,373,184 miles (9,460,730,472,581 km). It is used as a measurement for distance in space.

Meteor
A meteoroid that travels through Earth's atmosphere, leaving a streak of light as it burns up.

Meteorite
A meteor that hits the ground.

Meteoroid
Small particles of metal or stone that travel through space. Most come from asteroids broken apart by collisions with other asteroids.

Methane
A colorless, odorless gas. It is the principal component of natural gas used for cooking and heating homes.

Moon
A round body that orbits a planet.

Molten
Melted by extreme heat. Many planets and moons have molten rock at their center.

Nebula
A gas cloud that is the remains of an exploded star.

Orbit
The path of a celestial body or an artificial satellite as it revolves around another body.

Photosphere
The bright outer layer of the Sun.

Planet
A large, round body that orbits a star.

Red dwarf star
A cool, very faint star about half the size of our Sun. Red dwarfs are the most common type of star in the universe.

Solar flare
A sudden violent explosion of energy that occurs in the Sun's atmosphere near a sunspot.

Solar nebula
A cloud of dust and gas from which stars and planets form.

Solar prominence
An arc of gas between two sunspots. Prominences can loop hundreds of thousands of miles into space from the Sun's surface.

Sun
The star that is the center of our solar system.

Sunspot
A dark marking on the Sun's surface caused by a magnetic storm. It appears dark because it is slightly cooler than the surrounding area.

Super Earth
A rocky extrasolar planet 1.5 to 2 times larger than Earth.

Supernova
A giant star that has grown old, run out of fuel to burn, and exploded, sending star materials out into space.

Terrestrial planet
One of a class of planets primarily composed of silicate rocks. Also known as a rocky planet. The terrestrial planets in our solar system are Mercury, Venus, Earth, and Mars.

Compare your Earth weight with how much you'd weigh on other planets

Earth	Moon	Mercury	Venus	Mars	Ceres	Pluto	Haumea	Makemake	Eris
50/23	8/3.5	19/9	45/20	19/9	1.5/0.7	3/1.4	2.3/1	2.1/1	3.1/1.4
60/27	10/4.5	23/10	54/24	23/10	1.8/0.8	4/1.8	2.7/1.2	2.5/1.1	4.1/1.9
70/32	11.5/5.2	26/12	63/29	26/12	2.1/1	4.6/2.1	3.2/1.5	2.9/1.3	4.7/2.1
80/36	13/5.9	30/14	72/33	30/14	2.4/1.1	5.3/2.4	3.6/1.6	3.3/1.5	5.4/2.4
90/41	15/6.8	34/15	82/37	34/15	2.7/1.2	6/2.7	4.1/1.9	3.7/1.7	6.1/2.8
100/45	17/7.7	38/17	91/41	38/17	3/1.4	6.7/3	4.5/2	4.5/1.9	6.8/3.1

Jupiter, Saturn, Uranus, and Neptune are not included because they have no surface, so it would be impossible to stand on a scale to weigh yourself. The figures above are in pounds/kilograms.

Name	Mercury	Venus	Earth	Mars	Ceres	Jupiter
Meaning	Roman messenger of the gods	Roman goddess of love	Unknown	Roman god of war	Roman goddess of agriculture and of motherly love	Roman king of gods
Sun Position	1st	2nd	3rd	4th	5th	6th
Class of Planet	Rocky	Rocky	Rocky	Rocky	Dwarf	Gas Giant
Diameter	3,030 miles (4,878 km)	7,520 miles (12,100 km)	7,900 miles (12,750 km)	4,222 miles (6,794 km)	585 miles (940 km)	88,846 miles (142,984 km)
Density	5.43 g/cm³	5.25 g/cm³	5.52 g/cm³	3.94 g/cm³	2.08 g/cm³	1.30 g/cm³
Shape of Orbit	⬭	◯	◯	◯	◯	◯
Temperature	-300°F (-183°C) to 800°F (427°C)	864°F (462°C)	-126°F (-88°C) to 136°F (58°C)	-270°F (-133°C) to 80°F (27°C)	-159°F (-106°C)	-235°F (-150°C)
Number of Moons	none	none	1	2	none	at least 63
Rings	no	no	no	no	no	yes

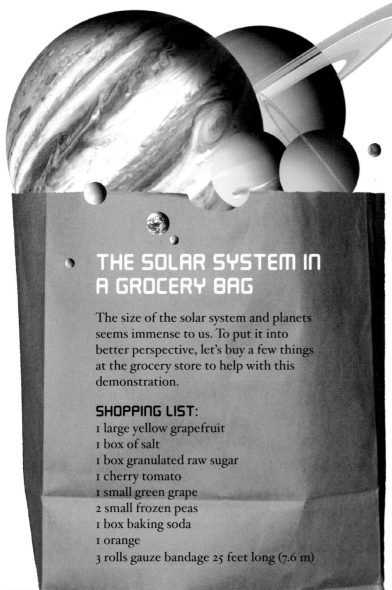

THE SOLAR SYSTEM IN A GROCERY BAG

The size of the solar system and planets seems immense to us. To put it into better perspective, let's buy a few things at the grocery store to help with this demonstration.

SHOPPING LIST:
1 large yellow grapefruit
1 box of salt
1 box granulated raw sugar
1 cherry tomato
1 small green grape
2 small frozen peas
1 box baking soda
1 orange
3 rolls gauze bandage 25 feet long (7.6 m)

If we use a grapefruit to represent our **Sun**, the planet **Mercury** will be the size of a small grain of salt, 18 feet (5.5 m) away from the grapefruit.

Venus will be larger than Mercury, about the size of a grain of raw sugar, located 34 feet (10.4 m) away.

Earth, also the size of a grain of raw sugar, will be 50 (15 m) feet away.

Mars, the size of a grain of salt, is 75 feet (23 m) away.

Ceres, a speck of dust, is located 150 feet (46 m) away.

Jupiter, a cherry tomato, is 240 feet (73 m) away.

Saturn, our green grape, is 420 feet (128 m) away.

Uranus, a frozen green pea, is 300 yards (274 m), or 3 football fields, away.

Neptune, another green pea, is 470 yards (430 m) away.

For **Pluto,** pick up a speck of baking soda and place it about 532 yards (486 m) away. (Pluto and the other dwarf planet orbits are not nice and round like the other planets. Their orbits are shaped like an egg so their distances from the Sun vary. (This measurement is an average of their orbits.)

Haumea is another speck of baking soda located around 570 yards (521 m) away.

Makemake is a piece of baking soda located another 612 yards (560 m) away.

Eris, your last piece of baking soda, located 900 yards (823 m) away. That's nine football fields long!

For a **Comet,** tie three rolls of gauze bandage together end-to-end to make one piece about 70 feet (22 m) long. This is the size of the Great Comet of 1843.

And what do we do with that orange? It represents **Proxima Centauri,** the nearest star to our Sun. Proxima Centauri is located 4.2 light-years away. To place it in proportion to our solar system, it would be about 2,400 miles (3,862 km) away from the grapefruit.

There you have it. This is our solar system (plus its neighboring star) to scale.

	Saturn	Uranus	Neptune	Pluto	Haumea	Makemake	Eris
	Roman god of agriculture	Greek god of the sky	Roman god of the sea	Roman god of the underworld	Hawaiian goddess of earth creatures	Easter Island god of life	Greek goddess of discord or confusion
	7th	8th	9th	10th	11th	12th	13th
	Gas Giant	Gas Giant	Gas Giant	Dwarf	Dwarf	Dwarf	Dwarf
	74,898 miles (120,536 km)	31,500 miles (50,724 km)	30,775 miles (49,528km)	1,430 miles (2,302 km)	1,218 x 943 miles (1,960 x 1,518 km)	466 miles (750 km)	1,678 miles (2,700km)
	0.70 g/cm³	1.24 g/cm³	1.76 g/cm³	2.03 g/cm³	2.6 g/cm³	2 g/cm³	2.1 g/cm³
	○	○	○	○	○	○	○
	-288°F (-178°C)	-323°F (-200°C)	-353°F (-214°C)	-369°F (-223°C)	-369F (-223°C)	-405F (-242°C)	-406°F (-243°C)
	at least 60	27	13	3	2	0	1
	yes	yes	yes	no	no	no	no

ACKNOWLEDGMENTS

I want to dedicate this book to all the young readers who love to draw alien worlds and dream of traveling to the stars. The Universe just called and left a message. Hurry up and join us out here! It is also dedicated to Becky Baines for her perseverance and razor-sharp editing; David Seager for his good cheer and artistic genius; Nancy Feresten for her unwavering confidence; Jeff Reynolds for his dynamite promotion of my works; Dr. Owen Gingerich, emeritus Harvard-Smithsonian astronomer, cosmic historian and good friend; Dr. Lisa Kaltenneger, exoplanet expert and excellent explainer of Neptunian orbits; Dr. Dimitar Sasselov, Director of the Harvard Origins of Life Initiative, for his clarity and vision; and this is dedicated especially to the Amazing Ms. Shirley–my wife–whose imaginative love flows through the pages of all my books. So my young readers, the planets are now in order. We've visited the Super Stars in the Milky Way. Where would you like to go next?

FURTHER EXPLORATION

Here are some great Web sites that you can visit to learn more about the new solar system.

Calculate your weight and age in the solar system
http://www.exploratorium.edu/ronh/weight/

Fun Solar System Activities
http://science.hq.nasa.gov/kids/solar_system.html
http://www.kidsastronomy.com/fun/make-a-solar-system.htm
http://spaceplace.nasa.gov/en/kids/sse_flipflop.shtml

Hubble Site
http://hubblesite.org/

Author's Site
www.aspenskies.com

Astronomy Magazine Site
http://www.astronomy.com/asy/default.aspx

Sky & Telescope Magazine Site
http://www.skyandtelescope.com/

Astronomy Picture of the Day
http://apod.nasa.gov/apod/

Space.com
http://www.space.com/news/

Harvard-Smithsonian Center for Astrophysics
http://cfa-www.harvard.edu/

INDEX

Boldface indicates illustrations.

Asteroid belt 11, **30**, 31
Asteroids 17, 31, **31**
Astronauts 22, 27, **27**, 58

Callisto (moon of Jupiter) 34, **34**, **35**
Ceres (dwarf planet) **10**, 11, 13, **30**, 31, 58, 59
Charon (moon of Pluto) **44**, 45
Comets 52, **52**, **53**, 59

Deimos (moon of Mars) **26**, 27
Dwarf planets 11, 12, 13, **13**, 51
Dysnomia (moon of Eris) 50, 51

Earth **20**, 21
  end of 54
  fact box 58
  Moon **2**, **20**, 22, **22**, 23, **23**
  relative size **10**, 59
  seasons 21, **21**
  in solar system 10, **13**
  Easter Island, South Pacific Ocean 49, **49**
Enceladus (moon of Saturn) 38, **38**
Eris (dwarf planet) 11, 11, 13, 50, 51, 59
Eros (asteroid) **31**
Europa (moon of Jupiter) **32**, 33, 34, **34**, **35**
Extrasolar planets 12, 56, **56**

Galileo 34
Ganymede (moon of Jupiter) 34, **34**, **35**
Gas giant planets 11, 12, 13, 13

Haumea (dwarf planet) 11, **11**, **46**, 47, 59
Hydra (moon of Pluto) **44**, 45

Iapetus (moon of Saturn) 38, **38**
Io (moon of Jupiter) 34, **34**, 35

Jupiter (planet) **32**, 33, **33**
  fact box 58
  moons **32**, 33, 34, **34**, **35**
  in night sky **2**
  relative size **10**, 59
  in solar system 11, **13**, 47

Kuiper Belt 11, **46**, 47, 47, **51**, 51

Lowell, Percival 45

Makemake (dwarf planet) 11, **11**, **48**, 49, 59
Mars (planet) **26**, 27
  fact box 58
  in night sky **2**
  relative size **10**, 59
  in solar system 10, 13
  water 28, 28, 29
Mercury (planet) **16**, 17, **17**
  crossing sun **14**
  fact box 58
  in night sky **3**
  relative size **10**, 59
  in solar system 10, **13**
Meteorites 24, **24–25**
Meteoroids 24
Meteors 24
Mimas (moon of Saturn) **36**, 38, **38**
Miranda (moon of Uranus) **40**, 41
Moons
  of Earth **2**, **20**, 22, **22**, 23, **23**
  of Eris **50**, 51
  of Jupiter **32**, 33, 34, **34**, **35**
  of Mars **26**, 27
  of Neptune **42**, 43
  of Pluto **44**, 45
  of Saturn **36**, 37, 38, **38**, **39**
  of Uranus **40**, 41

Neptune (planet) **42**, 43
  fact box 59
  in night sky **3**
  relative size **11**, 59
  in solar system 11, **13**, 47
Nix (moon of Pluto) **44**, 45

Oort Cloud 52, **52**

Phobos (moon of Mars) **26**, 27

Planetesimals 12, **12**
Pluto (dwarf planet) **11**, 13, **44**, 45, **45**, 59
Proxima Centauri (star) 52, **52**, 59

Saturn (planet) **36**, 37
  fact box 59
  moons **36**, 37, 38, **38**, **39**
  in night sky **2**
  relative size **11**, 59
  rings **36**, 37, **37**
  in solar system 11, 13, 47
Seasons 21, **21**
Solar flares **14**, 15, **15**
Solar system (ours) 10–11, **10–11**
  end of 54, 55
  formation of 12, **12**
  in a grocery bag 59
Solar systems (others) 12, 56, **56**, **56–57**
Sun **14**, 15
  end of 54, **55**
  formation of 12
  lifespan 54
  in night sky **2**
  parts of **15**
  relative size **10–11**, 11, 59
  in solar system 10, **13**, 47
Super-Earths 56, **56–57**

Terrestrial planets 10, 12, 13, **13**
Titan (moon of Saturn) 38, **38**, **39**
Tombaugh, Clyde 45
Triton (moon of Neptune) **42**, 43

Uranus (planet) **40**, 41, **41**
  fact box 59
  in night sky **3**
  relative size **11**, 59
  in solar system 11, **13**, 47

Venus (planet) **18**, 19
  fact box 58
  in night sky 3
  relative size **10**, 59
  in solar system 10, **13**

Weight, on each planet 58